LIFE DURING THE GREAT CIVILIZATIONS

The Celts

Other titles in the Life During the Great Civilizations series include:

Ancient Greece
Ancient Persia
Ancient Rome
The Aztec Empire
The Byzantine Empire
The Han Dynasty
The Inca
The Maya
The Mongol Empire
The Ottoman Empire
The Song Dynasty
The Vikings

LIFE DURING THE GREAT CIVILIZATIONS

The Celts

Sheila Wyborny

BLACKBIRCH PRESS
An imprint of Thomson Gale, a part of The Thomson Corporation

THOMSON / GALE

© 2005 Thomson Gale, a part of the Thomson Corporation.

Thomson and Star Logo are trademarks and Gale and Blackbirch Press are registered trademarks used herein under license.

For more information, contact
Blackbirch Press
27500 Drake Rd.
Farmington Hills, MI 48331-3535
Or you can visit our Internet site at http://www.gale.com

ALL RIGHTS RESERVED
No part of this work covered by the copyright hereon may be reproduced or used in any form or by any means—graphic, electronic, or mechanical, including photocopying, recording, taping, Web distribution or information storage retrieval systems—without the written permission of the publisher.

Every effort has been made to trace the owners of copyrighted material.

LIBRARY OF CONGRESS CATALOGING-IN-PUBLICATION DATA

Wyborny, Sheila, 1950–
  The Celts / by Sheila Wyborny.
    p. cm. — (Life during the great civilizations)
  Includes bibliographical references and index.
  ISBN 1-4103-0583-X (hardcover : alk. paper)
  1. Celts—Juvenile literature. 2. Civilization, Celtic—Juvenile literature. I. Title. II. Series.

D70.W93 2005
940'.04916—dc22   2004030121

Printed in United States
10 9 8 7 6 5 4 3 2 1

Contents

INTRODUCTION 7
    An Ancient Culture

CHAPTER ONE 9
    A Powerful Society

CHAPTER TWO 17
    Religion in Celtic Life

CHAPTER THREE 25
    Medicine, Technology, and Tools

CHAPTER FOUR 33
    Daily Life

NOTES 43

GLOSSARY 44

FOR MORE INFORMATION 45

INDEX 46

PICTURE CREDITS 47

ABOUT THE AUTHOR 48

INTRODUCTION

An Ancient Culture

At one time the Celts were one of Europe's major cultures. Historians and archaeologists agree that the Celts were a strong and powerful people. About twenty-two hundred years ago the Celts controlled much of what is now Europe. Their realm extended from Ireland and Britain in the north to Spain, France, and northern Italy in the south and eastward to Turkey and the Balkans. The Celts were not ruled by one king or emperor but by many chieftains. They were united by language and culture rather than government.

During the height of their civilization the Celts had no written language. Much of what is now known about the early Celts is from written records of other civilizations, such as the Romans and the Greeks. Since the lifestyle of the Celts was so different from that of the Greeks and the Romans, the Celts were thought to be uncivilized; in fact, the word *Celt* comes from the Greek word *Keltoi*, which means "barbarian." Consequently, Greek and Roman accounts of Celts were often not very flattering. Julius Caesar commented on the physical appearance of the Celtic warriors when he and his Roman troops attacked the British Isles: "All the Britons dye their bodies with woad, which produces a blue color and gives them a wild appearance in battle."[1]

This badly weathered sculpture shows a Celtic warrior with loot he has taken from the battlefield.

In this painting, Celtic warriors gather around a campfire on the coast of Gaul, in present-day France.

In addition to written accounts, artifacts also provide clues about Celtic society, religion, and everyday life. The early Celtic people buried weapons and tools in graves with their chieftains, and some of these burial sites, like Hallstatt in Austria, dated around 800 B.C., have been excavated. From these writings and artifacts, archaeologists and historians have learned much about the ancient Celtic people.

CHAPTER ONE

A Powerful Society

Despite what the Greeks and Romans thought of them, the Celts were not barbarians. In fact, Celtic society was well organized with highly skilled craftsmen and clearly defined roles among the classes. Celtic society, its religion, and its craftsmanship developed over thousands of years.

History of the Celts

Many scientists believe that the Celts descended from two groups, each named for artifacts they left behind. One group of people originated in what is now southern Russia. These people, called the Battle Axe People, spread across the continent into central, western, and northwestern Europe. In central Europe, the Battle Axe People united with a group called the Beaker Folk, a group known to have lived in central Europe as far back as 3000 B.C. These groups evolved into the Celts, and by 800 B.C. Celtic civilization flourished from England to the Alps. The Celts continued to dominate much of Europe until about 300 B.C., when the combined efforts of the Romans, Germans, and Greeks forced the Celts to retreat. By A.D. 100, Great Britain was the only area still controlled by the Celts.

Although the British Isles are the countries most associated with the Celts, two very important early Celtic settlements were located in other countries. One of these settlements is Hallstatt, in Austria. A mining community, Hallstatt thrived between 1200 and

Artifacts like this bronze boar discovered at the La Tène site in Switzerland provide a wealth of knowledge about Celtic civilization.

475 B.C. The remains of Hallstatt were discovered in the early 1800s. During its excavation, the Hallstatt archaeological site yielded over a thousand graves with an abundance of grave goods and a wealth of other early Iron Age artifacts, such as tools, weapons, brooches, pins, and even bits of fabric. In fact, while excavating a Celtic salt mine site in the region, archaeologists uncovered the perfectly preserved remains of an ancient Celtic miner.

Another important archaeological site was discovered in the mid-1800s. This settlement, called the La Tène site, is located on the northern side of Lake Neuchâtel in Switzerland. Dredging began in the 1860s, when archaeologists discovered an area where ancient timbers, believed to be the remains of lake dwellings, were driven into the lake bed. Between the 1860s and the 1880s, the lake yielded a rich trove of artifacts left behind by the ancient Celts. These items include shields, spearheads, swords, razors, belt clasps, bronze cauldrons, and human remains. Some archaeologists believe that these artifacts were cast into the lake during rituals, and that the La Tène site was some sort of religious sanctuary. Others believe it was a trade center. Whichever the case, La Tène and Hallstatt have provided a wealth of knowledge about the Celtic civilization and glimpses into the lives of the early Celts.

Celtic Society

Celtic society was composed of four main groups; nobles, warriors, scholars, and farmers. In some instances, though, these groups overlapped. Tribal rulers, or chieftains, were the wealthiest group. Some chieftains were nobles while others were great warriors who had distinguished themselves in battle. Many chieftains inherited their titles from their fathers, but others were selected by a council of nobles. Chieftains enjoyed making a great show of their wealth and were extremely generous to guests, serving lavish banquets and expensive wines.

Celtic civilization began in what is now central Europe and expanded across the continent.

Although most tribal chieftains were men, some tribes were ruled by women. As a whole, Celtic women enjoyed a greater degree of equality than their Greek and Roman counterparts and had some influence in the governing of their tribes.

The largest group in Celtic society were the farmers. Many farmers were needed to raise enough food to feed all of the members of Celtic society. Farmers raised mostly grains, like wheat, rye, barley, and oats, but they also raised beans and lentils. The Greek geographer Strabo describes the wealth of crops grown by the Celts: "All the rest of the country produces grain in large quantities, and millet, and nuts, and all kinds of livestock."[2]

Some of the wealthier farmers were members of the scholar class. The scholars were the educated class of Celtic society and served in a variety of roles. Some were doctors or holy men, called Druids. Others were skilled craftsmen such as metal workers. Scholars were also responsible for learning the history, stories, and poetry of the tribes and passing them down to the next generation.

Most Celts were farmers. This bronze statuette found at Hallstatt shows a farmer with a team of oxen yoked to his plow.

The next group, the warriors, belonged to two classes, the farmers and the nobility. On the fields of battle, the noble warriors and the farmer warriors were easy to identify. Noble warriors had finely crafted swords, shields, and body armor, while the farmer warriors had no body armor and weapons that were not as fine. In fact, farmer warriors often surged onto the battlefield wearing only body paint.

Slaves were also a part of the Celtic culture, but they had no rights or privileges in society. Slaves were members of enemy tribes captured by Celtic warriors in battle. The Celts used slaves for labor and also traded them to the Romans for wine. Wine was so valuable to the Celts that the rate of exchange was one slave for one bottle of wine.

In addition to these classes, there were other divisions in Celtic social structure. For instance, young teenage males who no longer needed the care of their families tended to band together. Some of these young men trained to be warriors and others learned crafts and skills that would support them and their families when they became adults. These craftsmen were valued members of Celtic society.

Crafts, Skills, and Trades

The Celts were talented craftsmen. Woodworkers, for example, were skilled in the use of woodworking tools such as saws, lathes, and adzes to create tool handles, buckets, barrels, and even ornately carved bowls. Examples of their work have been found in ancient graves and other archaeological sites.

The Celts were also gifted metalworkers. They made basic items such as spearheads and tools. They also made more elaborate items, including bowls made of bronze and silver and decorated inside and out with geometric patterns, trees, plants, or human and animal figures. Other decorative items included masks, belt clasps, and jewelry.

Symbols in Celtic Art

Symbols were a part of both Celtic art and culture. One of the most popular symbols was the spiral. To the Celts, spirals had several meanings. A single spiral turned in a clockwise direction represented the winter sun. A counter-clockwise spiral symbolized the summer sun. The triple spiral, three spirals arranged in a triangular shape, had special meaning for the Celts. It symbolized mind, body, and spirit.

Animals and trees were also popular symbols in Celtic art. Deer and horses represented hunting. The snake, a creature that sheds its skin, was a symbol of rebirth. Any tree design was considered to hold great power.

Horses like this one decorating an axe frequently appear in Celtic art as a symbol of hunting.

These symbols were used in jewelry, embroidered into clothing, carved into stone, and crafted into sword hilts and vessels such as decorative bowls. Examples of these symbols have been found in Celtic graves and on ancient stone monuments.

This panel from an elaborate silver bowl is thought to show a Celtic god.

The Celts were especially skilled jewelry makers. One piece they made was the fibula, a clasp for securing clothing similar to a safety pin. Jewelers also crafted more elaborate pins, called brooches, in gold and silver. Some brooches were inlaid with semiprecious stones and coral. Bracelets, necklaces, and rings were popular jewelry items as well.

Metalworkers made heavy gold necklaces, called torques, which were worn by nobles and warriors as symbols of their status. Other items the craftsmen made for noble warriors were elaborately decorated helmets, shields with swirling patterns, and sword hilts inlaid with stones.

Additionally, the Celts were skilled weavers. They favored stripes and plaids in bold colors that were created from vegetable dyes. The clothing of nobles was decorated with fine embroidery. Women did the weaving, embroidery, and sewing.

Artifacts left behind by the Celts prove their skills as craftsmen and provide other clues about Celtic civilization. Some of the symbols used to decorate jewelry, bowls, and shields were connected to the religious beliefs and mythology of the Celts.

CHAPTER TWO

Religion in Celtic Life

Religion was an important part of daily life to the ancient Celts. A society so strongly linked to religion required a specially trained group of people to lead them in their religious ceremonies and events and interpret the wills of their gods and goddesses. These religious leaders were called Druids.

The Druids

Druid priests were powerful and influential people. In fact, in Celtic society the priests often had more power and influence than the chieftains, because the Celtic people believed that Druid priests could communicate directly with the gods. Julius Caesar writes about the power of the Druids: "The Druids are in charge of religion. They have control over public and private sacrifices and give rulings on all religious questions. Large numbers of young men go to them for instruction and they are greatly honored by the people."[3] Since they would become so powerful in Celtic society, candidates for priesthood were usually recruited from the noble class.

Becoming a Druid priest was a long and involved process. A young boy might begin his training at ten or twelve and continue his studies until he was in his thirties. The early Celts had no written language, so none of their education came from books. Since they had no books for reference, the student priests had to commit all of their ceremonies to memory.

In this painting, an old Druid wearing white robes and gold jewelry performs a ritual.

A Druid pours an offering to the gods as men prepare a cow for sacrifice.

    In addition to studying religion, Druid priests had to learn a wide variety of other topics. They had to memorize all of the laws, rules, lore, legends, and rituals of their tribes. This is because they were not only the religious leaders of their tribes, but also the teachers, mathematicians, lawyers, astronomers, and healers. The Druid priests even had the responsibility of deciding when their tribes went to war. This was not all the priests did, though.

    Additional responsibilities included maintaining the Celtic calendar, choosing dates for festivals, and determining which days would be lucky for conducting business. One duty of the Druids was particularly gruesome. Druid priests conducted sacrifices of both animals and humans to please their gods. Human victims were often captives of war or people who had committed crimes against the community, like robbery. Priests killed these sacrificial victims with swords, arrows, or spears. Following the sacrifice the remains were burned on piles of straw and wood.

Other priestly responsibilities were not so violent. Druid priests were thought to have magical powers. The Celts believed their priests could predict the future and turn themselves into animals. They also believed that the Druids could levitate and predict weather.

Sacred Places and Objects

The priests did not actually predict weather or turn themselves into animals, but they did have close links with nature. Many trees, plants, and natural surroundings held a sacred place in the Druid religion. The Druids believed that the trees were the dwelling places of tree spirits as well as home to spirits of the dead. All trees were sacred, but the oak tree was the most revered of all trees. According to the Celts, the oak held the doorway to the otherworld, the home of mythical beings and

A Druid and a band of warriors give thanks to the gods after they find mistletoe, one of the most sacred plants to the Celts.

supernatural monsters. In fact, the Celtic word for oak is *daur*, which means "door," and the word *Druid* derives from this word.

Since trees were sacred, woodlands were hallowed places. The Druids preferred natural woodlands to temples, and so they worshipped their gods and goddesses in sacred groves called *nemetons*. The Druids furnished these woodland groves with altars carved with images of tree spirits.

Plants other than trees were also sacred to the Druids. One of the most sacred plants was mistletoe. The Celtic word for mistletoe means "all heal." The Druids believed that mistletoe had many magical powers and was connected to the soul of the tree in which it grew. They believed mistletoe cured diseases, protected people from witchcraft, made poisons harmless, and brought good luck. Mistletoe was so sacred that if enemies inadvertently met beneath it in the forest, they put down their weapons and stopped fighting for an entire day.

Votive figures like this man in a boat were typically carved from rock crystal or white quartz and were believed to protect Celtic warriors in battle.

The Druids held a special mistletoe ceremony five days after the first new moon following the winter solstice. Using a golden sickle, they cut mistletoe from the sacred oaks, divided it into sprigs, and distributed it among the people to ward off evil. This was the origin of today's tradition of hanging mistletoe over the door at Christmastime.

Like trees and plants, water was sacred to the Druids. Water comes from the earth, so the Druids associated it with their goddess Earth Mother. The Druids believed their goddesses lived in natural water sources, like springs, lakes, and pools. They believed these goddesses could protect warriors in battle and heal the sick. To ask help from the water goddesses, the Druids threw votives into the water. Votives were figures carved from rock crystal or white quartz, minerals believed to be favored by the goddesses. This was but one of the many ceremonies the Celts and their Druid priests participated in throughout the year.

Ceremonies and Rituals

The Celts had many seasonal festivals to honor their gods and goddesses. Samhain (pronounced SOW-win) was held October 31 through November 1. Samhain was the Feast of the Dead and the beginning of the Celtic New Year. The Celts believed that the boundary between their world and the otherworld was at its thinnest at this time. This was a time to communicate with the spirit world and to predict the future. The Celts decorated their homes with jack-o'-lanterns and sprigs of holly, which symbolized rebirth, and celebrated with bonfires, feasts, and games honoring the dead.

The next important celebration was the winter solstice, also called Yule, which occurs around December 22. The winter solstice, the shortest day of the year, was a celebration of new beginnings, when light reentered the world and days began to lengthen again. It was a time to resolve problems and issues of the past, to forgive and forget,

Musical Instruments

For festivals and celebrations the Celts accompanied their music with instruments. One of their earliest instruments is the harp. The Celtic harp is much smaller than harps that are played in most orchestras today.

In addition to the harp, the Celts had a one-sided drum called a bodhran. *Bodhran* is a Celtic word for tray. According to one story, the Celts had round, skin-covered trays among their household goods. One day someone noticed the rhythmic sound the tray made when it was thumped. Later, drummers used a thick stick called a tipper to play the drum. The bodhran and the harp are still played today in Irish concerts, festivals, and heritage celebrations in the British Isles and other places.

Another ceremonial instrument was a long trumpetlike horn, made of beaten bronze, called a carnyx. In addition to its use during ceremonies, the carnyx was blown to lead troops into battle. The bell end of the horn was shaped like the head of an animal, such as a boar. The carnyx dates back to 300–200 B.C.

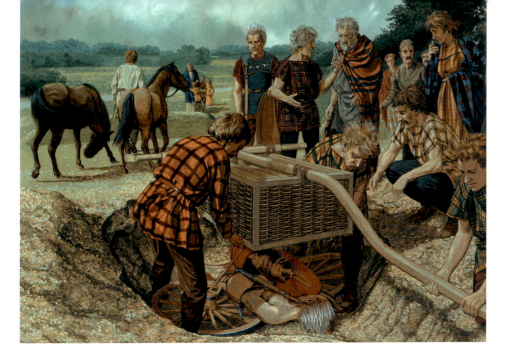

A group of warriors buries a comrade slain in battle with his belongings at his side.

and to look to the future with optimism. At this time the Celts decorated their homes with holly and burned yule logs, which were huge logs, sometimes entire trees. These logs were slowly fed to the fire throughout the celebration.

Another celebration, Beltane, occurred May 1. This was a time people gave thanks for the arrival of spring. The Celts believed that Beltane was the best day to celebrate weddings, because it was a time of life and birth. Communities lit two bonfires and young people leaped over the fires for good luck. The Celts also danced around tall poles in honor of Beltane. This celebration was the origin of dancing around the maypole.

Funeral ceremonies were another important Celtic ritual. The Celts believed in life after death, and so funerals, especially those of the noble class, were significant events. The Celts buried or cremated the earthly remains of their dead. Julius Caesar describes this practice: "Funerals are splendid and costly. Everything the dead man is thought to have been fond of is put on the pyre, including animals. Not long ago, slaves and dependants known to have been their master's favorites were burned with them at the end of the funeral."[4] After the cremation fires died out, the remains were placed in pots or urns. Cremated remains were also placed in tombs or graves. Since the Celts believed in an afterlife, they placed favorite belongings, such as jewelry, tools, dishes, and other household items, in the graves of the deceased for use in the next world. The graves of some of the more important nobles also contained furniture, wagons, and wines.

As archaeologists and other scientists examined ancient Celtic gravesites, they learned much about Celtic society and religious beliefs. Some of the items found in the graves also provided clues about how the Celts practiced medicine and developed tools and other devices.

CHAPTER THREE

Medicine, Technology, and Tools

The Celts were quite advanced in science and technology for their time and had a number of labor-saving devices for household chores. The Celts mined metals and minerals and possessed the technology to strengthen metals into strong and effective tools and weapons. They also practiced medicine.

Medicines and Healing

The Celts cared for the old, the sick, and the injured. They operated hospitals where they treated illness, performed surgery, and attended to the needs of the elderly who could no longer care for themselves.

The Celts thought illness was a punishment for angering their gods, so they treated it with a combination of magic and herbal medicine. While the magic portion of their medical treatments was sometimes nothing more than burning certain herbs in spell-making rituals or casting votives into sacred bogs, human and animal sacrifice could also be a part of the healing process.

Healers did more than perform spells and appeal to their gods, though. They set broken bones and practiced primitive surgical techniques, like trephining. Trephining is the process of boring a hole in the skull with a sawlike device in an effort to treat head injuries. Some patients survived the ordeal, but many died from shock. Surgical tools such as probes, retractors, and trephining saws have been discovered at archaeological sites.

A relief found in Scotland shows two Celtic figures with axes slung over their shoulders.

Celtic healers were also skilled in the use of medicinal herbs. They understood the healing properties of hundreds of plants and used herbs to treat nearly every health problem. A number of herbs had several uses. For instance, comfrey was used to relieve pain, cure fever, and stop bleeding. Catnip and willow were also used as pain relievers. Marigold was applied to skin irritations, and mistletoe and foxglove were used to stimulate the heart. Celtic healers made antiseptics from bilberry, heather, and lavender and cured headaches with willow bark

This is a gold replica of the single-mast boat the Celts used on long ocean journeys.

or wintergreen. Upset stomachs were soothed with teas made from peppermint or ginger, and hawthorne and mistletoe were used to treat high blood pressure. Chickweed, fennel, and garlic provided relief for respiratory illnesses.

Tools, Weapons, and Travel

The Celts were knowledgeable in the use of herbs to treat disorders and cure illness, but their advanced skills were not limited to the practice of medicine. The Celts developed several types of transportation, both land and sea. If they needed to travel a short distance over level terrain, the Celts used large, four-wheel wagons pulled by a yoked pair of horses. After a short time, however, the yokes became too uncomfortable for the horses, so for long distances the Celts traveled and moved goods by boat.

For these long journeys the Celts had large single-mast wooden boats with leather sails and iron anchor cables. To allow them to be either rowed or sailed, these boats were outfitted with several pairs of oars. These ships are described by Julius Caesar: "The [Celts] own ships were built in a different way from ours. . . . They used sails made of hides or soft leather either because flax was scarce or they did not know how to use it, or more probably because they thought that with cloth sails they would not be able to withstand the forces of the violent Atlantic gales, or steer such heavy ships."[5]

A boat called a coracle was used for traveling short distances by water. Coracles were round or oval shaped. Their frames were made from wicker and were covered with animal skins. Coracles were very light and could be easily lifted over obstacles or carried overland.

While boats and carts were sufficient for peacetime travel, the Celts needed swifter transportation in times of war. For battle and hunting, the Celts had light, swift, two-wheel carts called chariots. The chariot had a flat wooden bottom and wicker side panels to protect its two occupants, the driver and the warrior. A pole with a yoke connected the chariot to a pair of horses. The fronts of the chariots were left open so the warrior could easily leap out onto the pole and fight enemy soldiers.

In addition to effective transportation, the Celts had several labor-saving devices. One such device was the rotating quern, or hand mill, first used in about 200 B.C. Before this time grains were ground in a saddle quern, a large flat stone with a cylindrical or round grinding stone. With the saddle quern, grinding was a slow, tedious process of pounding or grinding by hand. A rotating quern consisted of two round stones. The grain was poured into the hole in the center of the top stone. The bottom stone had a depression to keep the flour and grain from spilling over the sides. As the top stone was turned by a handle, the grain ran through the hole onto the bottom stone where it was ground into flour. With a saddle quern, it took a person an hour to grind a pound of flour. With the rotating quern, however, a pound of flour could be ground in about five minutes.

This panel from a bronze bowl shows a charioteer in the heat of a race. The Celts used chariots primarily for hunting and in battle.

    The Celts also had large looms. The warp-weighted loom enabled weavers to make strips of fabric up to sixty inches wide. The top of the warp-weighted loom frame was a heavy roller beam. The warp yarns, or stationary vertical yarns, were attached to this top beam and weighted at the bottom with weights made of fired clay or stone. Some of these weights were triangular in shape with holes for the warp yarn at each corner. That way, if one corner of the weight broke, the weight could still be used by tying the warp yarn at another corner. The weft yarn, or horizontal yarn, was wound on shuttles and woven in and out of these warp yarns and then tapped into place.

    The Celts fashioned garments from metal in addition to woven cloth. Celtic warriors of the noble class were fortunate to have special protection that some historians say is a purely Celtic invention. Chain mail was first seen on the battlefield after 300 B.C. Weighing nearly 35

Celtic Alphabet

During the height of their civilization, the Celts had no written language. Many historians believe that the Celts did not develop a written language until sometime between the first and the third centuries A.D. During this period of time, the Druids developed an alphabet whose letters are composed of one to five vertical or angled lines crossing a horizontal midline. Unlike the English alphabet, this alphabet is read from the bottom up.

Called ogham in honor of the Celtic god Ogma, the Celtic alphabet was composed of twenty characters. These characters were named for sacred trees. For example, the letter *A* stood for *ailim*, a word meaning "elm," the letter *B* was for *bithe*, or "birch." The Celtic alphabet also had symbols for vine, reed, and feather.

Over three hundred examples of these Celtic writings survive today. They are found on standing stones mostly in Ireland, but others are scattered around Scotland, England, and Wales. Celtic writing has also been found in ivory, bronze, bone, and silver artifacts.

pounds, chain mail, made of many interlocking metal rings, was fashioned into long tunics and hoods. Warriors who wore chain mail had added protection from knife cuts and sword blows. This chain mail was made from metals mined by the Celts.

Mining Technology

The Celts mined metals and forged them into superior tools, weapons, and armor. Two of the metals they mined were copper and iron ore. Iron was easier to mine than copper because iron was mined near the Earth's surface in wooded areas and wetlands, whereas copper mining involved digging deep shafts into the ground. After the ores were mined, they were smelted. Smelting is a process that uses a very hot furnace to separate iron from other materials in the ore. The extreme heat separates the pure iron, which falls into a lump at the bottom of the furnace. When the furnace cooled, the pure iron was removed and fashioned into tools and weapons.

This illustration shows two Celtic warriors, one dressed only in animal skins, and the other wearing protective gear, including chain mail.

The Celts also mined salt. Some of the best quality salt was mined in the mountains near Hallstatt. To get to the salt, miners carved sloping shafts into the mountains using large picks. From the shafts, the miners dug tunnels into the salt deposits. Although it was very dangerous work, the Celts were able to mine enough salt for their own needs and to trade with other groups.

Salt was an extremely valuable mineral. There was no refrigeration to keep stored meats and other foods from spoiling, so the Celts and other cultures preserved them by putting them in barrels of salt.

Without a way to preserve food to eat between harvest seasons and during the harshest winter weather when the men could not hunt, the people would have starved.

The Celts made good use of the resources in their environment and their labor-saving devices and technology. These skills and technologies enabled Celtic civilization to prosper for hundreds of years as Celtic families passed along the skills and knowledge of their civilization from generation to generation.

CHAPTER FOUR

Daily Life

The basic units of Celtic life were the family and the clan. The word *clan*, or *clann*, is a Celtic word meaning children. Clan families were all related to a common ancestor and clansmen were fiercely loyal to one another, devoting long workdays to supporting their families and protecting their communities.

Family Structure

A family household consisted of a man, his wife, and the man's extended family. This extended family included elderly parents, aunts, and uncles. Family ties were very strong and family members supported one another. The Celts had an unusual method of raising children, though. Children were given to foster parents to raise. The foster father was usually a married brother of the child's mother.

Since there were no schools, children spent their days with their foster families. As soon as they were old enough, they helped with family tasks. They weeded gardens and scared away birds and animals that were harmful to crops. They also helped prepare wool for spinning into yarn by combing out tangles and removing debris. Older boys and girls helped grind wheat into flour for bread.

Usually, chores were defined by sex. Women did the cooking, weaving, sewing, and other housework. The men built the houses, hunted for game, and defended the villages. When crops were ready for harvest, however, everyone in the village—men, women, and children—helped in the fields. Another shared task was grinding wheat into flour. Since

The Celtic family unit consisted of a man, his wife, and the man's extended family.

so much bread was needed to feed all of the families in the community, the task of grinding wheat fell to any men or women who were not involved in other tasks.

Homes and Communities

In addition to sharing responsibilities, the Celts worked to maintain their settlements. These settlements were called *oppida*. By the first century B.C. the Celts had learned how to build drainage systems and pave roads, so the *oppida* were relatively clean, modern communities. For defense, *oppida* were built on high hills or plateaus, so the residents had a wide view of the surrounding territory. *Oppida* were

These wattle and daub huts at a national park in Ireland were reconstructed to look like typical Celtic homes.

The interior of a Celtic home consisted of one large room that was used for cooking, eating, and sleeping.

surrounded by earthen walls that were fortified with stone and topped with palisades, high wooden fences built from tall posts. A small *oppidum* might have contained just a few homes, but up to a thousand people lived in larger *oppida*.

Celtic homes in Britain and Ireland were usually round. Tall timbers were cut and trimmed to support the house. One end of the timbers was placed in holes in the ground. Cross pieces, also long timbers, were tied to the uprights to form the tops of the walls. The roof framework was made of wood lashed to the wall framework. The roof was steeply pitched so rainwater ran off rather than leaking into the inside of the house. Usually the walls were made of a woven twig framework plastered with thick mud. This technique is called wattle and daub.

Homes had one main room for sleeping, eating, and cooking. Benchlike platforms built along the walls and covered with furs were used for sleeping. Aside from these platforms the Celts had little furniture, and families stored their belongings under the sleeping platforms. The floors were hard-packed earth with a stone-lined fire pit in the center. Since the roofs were made of thatch, no smoke holes were needed. Smoke escaped through gaps in the thatched roofs.

Oppida had other types of buildings as well. The Celts built shelters for their animals and storehouses for grain and hay. Grain storehouses were built atop wooden platforms, which prevented mice and rats from getting into the grain. Additionally, the Celts built storage buildings for their farm equipment, chariots, and wagons.

Clothing and Jewelry

The citizens of the *oppida* favored bright colored clothing and jewelry. The women wore long loose gowns belted with strips of cloth or leather or sleeved tunics tucked into long skirts. These garments were woven from wool. In cool weather they added shawls, draped over their shoulders and fastened with a fibula. In warmer weather they wore leather sandals, and in winter they wore short boots tied at the ankle with narrow strips of leather. Women wore bracelets, finger and toe rings, and necklaces made of colorful glass beads.

Celtic women also wore cosmetics. They painted their nails, darkened their eyebrows with berry juice, and rouged their cheeks. Hairstyles were simple—a single braid, either worn down the back or twisted into a bun at the back of the head.

Celtic men had two styles of dress, depending on the region in which they lived. On the continental mainland they wore trousers, called *bracae*, and tunics. In the British Isles, however, they wore thigh-length belted tunics and cloaks. Like the women, the men wore

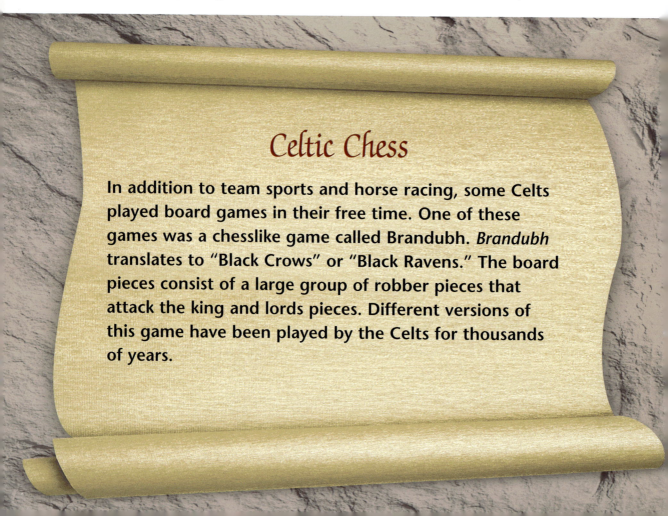

Celtic Chess

In addition to team sports and horse racing, some Celts played board games in their free time. One of these games was a chesslike game called Brandubh. *Brandubh* translates to "Black Crows" or "Black Ravens." The board pieces consist of a large group of robber pieces that attack the king and lords pieces. Different versions of this game have been played by the Celts for thousands of years.

Celtic men from the British Isles wore long, belted tunics, while mainland Celts dressed in trousers.

leather shoes. In winter, both men and women wore long-sleeved tunics and heavy woolen cloaks.

Children dressed in styles similar to their parents. It was not unusual for children to play outside in the coldest winter weather without their cloaks, however. Adults believed that allowing children to go about the village thinly clad in winter toughened them so they would become strong adults.

Leisure Activities

Another way children developed strength and coordination was by playing games. Hurling and shinty were two favorite team sports of the Celts. Both games are played with long sticks and small balls. As

This bronze relief shows two Celtic boxers in a match. The plumed helmet in the center is the prize for the winner.

in hockey, the objective of both games is to move the ball down the playing field to the opponent's goal. Adults and children both played shinty and hurling and both sports are popular in the British Isles today. Hurling is considered an Irish sport and shinty is played mostly in Scotland.

The Celts enjoyed other sports and games as well. Horse racing was popular, especially during the Lughnasadh games, held in late summer or early fall. In addition to horse racing, the Celts competed in archery, jousting, and tug-of-war during Lughnasadh. They also competed in other games, some similar to games and sports played in many countries today. Kayles, similar to bowling, was played with eight pins set inside a chalk circle. Competitors stood about fifteen feet from the circle and threw sticks at the pins. The objective was to knock down all of the pins. Another favorite game the Celts played was called rhibo. Variations of this game have been played for hundreds of years by many cultures. To play rhibo, three pairs of people clasped hands to form a "bed." Once the bed of arms was formed, a fourth person climbed aboard. The "bed" people threw this person as high into the air as they could. The game of rhibo symbolized throwing wheat into the air to separate it from the chaff. Finally, an energetic game called stick-jumping was popular with the Celts, but it was suitable only for the very agile. A person held a four-foot stick

An old coin shows a man horse racing, a sport the Celts enjoyed.

by both ends. The objective was to jump over the stick, lifting the knees as high as possible, without letting go of either end or falling to the ground.

The Celts were robust people, as creative with their sports and games as they were with their craftsmanship and technology. Evidence of their early influence can still be found in many places in western Europe, and the Celtic spirit lives on in the British Isles today.

Notes

Introduction: An Ancient Culture

1. Julius Caesar, *The Battle for Gaul*, trans. Anne Wise and Peter Wise. Boston: David R. Godine, 1980, p. 94.

Chapter 1: A Powerful Society

2. Strabo, *The Geography of Strabo,* trans. Horace Leonard Jones. London: William Heinemann, 1960, p. 169.

Chapter 2: Religion in Celtic Life

3. Caesar, *The Battle for Gaul*, p. 53.
4. Caesar, *The Battle for Gaul*, p. 124.

Chapter 3: Medicine, Technology, and Tools

5. Caesar, *The Battle for Gaul*, p. 64.

Glossary

bracae: A Latin word for pants or trousers.

clan: A number of families united by a common ancestor.

coracle: A small, round, lightweight, leather-covered boat the Celts used to travel short distances.

cremate: To burn human remains to ashes in extremely hot fires.

Druids: The holy men of the early Celts.

fibula: A type of early safety pin.

hallowed: Sacred or holy.

levitate: To rise without any visible means of support.

otherworld: The afterworld or spirit world of Celtic beliefs.

pallisade: A protective wall made from tall wooden poles.

quern: A carved stone used to grind corn or wheat into flour.

retractor: A surgical instrument used to hold back skin.

smelting: The process of heating ores in extremely hot furnaces until pure metal is separated from mineral.

torques: Heavy metal or golden necklaces. Worn by warriors, torques protected their necks in battle.

trephining: The process of removing a small section of the skull with a sawlike surgical tool.

votive: A small model made from stone or wood that the Celts offered to the gods and goddesses.

woad: An herb used to make blue dye.

For More Information

Books

Simon James, *The World of the Celts*. London: Thames and Hudson, 1993.

Katherine Hinds, *The Celts of Northern Europe*. New York: Benchmark, 1997.

Allison Lassieur, *The Celts*. San Diego, CA: Lucent, 2001.

Hazel Mary Martel, *The Celts*. New York: Penguin, 1994.

Sam McBratney, *Celtic Myths*. New York: Peter Bedrick, 1997.

Juliet Wood, *The Celts: Life, Myth, and Art*. London: HarperCollins, 1998.

Web Sites

Britain Express (www.britainexpress.com/History/Celtic_Britain.htm). This Web site explains who the Celts were and their origins. Additionally, it provides information about religion, daily life, and housing. Includes links to related sites.

Celtic Corner (www.celticcorner.com/origins.html). Beginning with the ancestry of the early Celtic culture, this site includes information on Celtic languages and the physical appearance of the Celts.

Celtic Grounds (www.celticgrounds.com/chapters). This site provides a wealth of information about the Celts, including customs, religion, tribes, jewelry, and much more.

Spirit Songs (www.spiritsongs.org/Ancient_Civilizations_Articles_Celtic_Civilization.htm). This site includes information on the origins of the Celts, their culture and religion, information about Druidic celebrations and festivals, and a time line of Celtic civilization.

Index

Afterlife, 24
Alphabet, 30
Art, 14

Battle Axe People, 9
Beaker Folk, 9
Boats, 27–28
Burial sites, 8, 10

Calendar, 18
Celebrations, 22
Ceremonies, 17, 21, 23–24
Chain mail, 29, 31
Chariots, 28
Chess, 38
Chieftains, 7, 8, 11, 17
Children, 33, 40
Clothing, 14, 15, 37–40
Communities, 35–37
Copper, 31
Craftsmen, 12, 13–15

Daily life, 17, 33–42
Death, 23–24
Druids, 12, 17–19, 30

Family, 33–35
Farmers, 11, 12, 13
Festivals, 18, 21, 22
Food, 32
Funerals, 23–24

Games, 38, 40–42

Grains, 12, 28

Hallstatt, 8, 9–10, 31
Healing, 25–27
Herbs, 25, 26
Homes, 35–37

Iron, 31

Jewelry, 14, 15, 37–40

Language, written, 7, 17, 30
La Tène, 10–11
Leisure activities, 40–42
Looms, 29

Magic, 25
Medicines, 25–27
Metals and metalworkers, 12, 13, 15, 25, 29, 31
Mining, 9, 25, 31–32
Mistletoe, 20–21
Music, 22

Nature, 19
Nemetons, 20
Nobles, 11, 13, 15, 17, 23, 24, 29

Plants, 20

Religion, 16–24

Rituals, 21, 23–24

Sacrifices, 17, 18–19, 25
Salt, 31
Scholars, 11, 12
Slaves, 13
Social structure, 11–13
Society, 9–15
Solstice, 21, 23
Spring, 23
Symbols, 14, 15

Technology, 25–32
Tools, 8, 27–31
Travel, 27–31
Trees, 14, 19–20

Votives, 21, 25

Warriors, 11, 13, 29
Water, 21
Weapons, 8, 27–31
Weavers, 15, 29
Weddings, 23
Wheat, 33, 35
Wine, 13, 21
Women, 12, 15, 33, 37
Woodworkers, 13

Picture Credits

Cover image: © Erich Lessing/Art Resource
© akg-images/Peter Connolly, 23, 31, 34
© Erich Lessing/Art Resource, NY, 6, 12, 14, 20, 29, 40
© HIP/Scala/Art Resource, NY, 16
© North Wind Pictures, 19, 39
© Réunion des Musées Nationaux/Art Resource, NY, 8, 10
© Stapleton Collection/CORBIS, 18
© Homer Sykes/CORBIS, 26
© Werner Forman/Art Resource, NY, 27
© Werner Forman/CORBIS, 15, 41
© Felix Zaska/CORBIS, 35, 36

About the Author

A retired teacher, Sheila Wyborny has been writing nonfiction books for children since 2000. She and her husband Wendell live on a small private airport near Houston, Texas, where they often fly their aircraft, a Cessna 170, from their own backyard.

18^{25}

940
WYB

The Celts.

30229012292552